I0794093

Scary States (of Mind)

Horror in Pennsylvania

by Joyce Markovics

Consultant: Debbie Felton
Professor of Classics
University of Massachusetts
Amherst, Massachusetts

Bearport Publishing
Minneapolis, Minnesota

Credits

Cover, © Kim Jones, © Sherman Cahal/Shutterstock, © Bogdan Sonjachnyj/Shutterstock, © Alik Mulikov/Shutterstock, © zhu difeng/Shutterstock, and © worapatpong rattanapan/Shutterstock; 3, © Scott Heaney/Shutterstock; 4-5, © Kim Jones, © Fotokvadrat/Shutterstock, © yevgeniy11/Shutterstock, and © f11photo/Shutterstock; 7, © John Bilous/Shutterstock; 7 inset, © Keith Lance/iStock; 8-9, © George Sheldon/Shutterstock and Courtesy Library of Congress; 10 , © Cory Seamer/Shutterstock; 11, © Alison Hancock/Shutterstock; 12, © duncan1890/iStock; 13, © MISHELLA/Shutterstock; 14 , © Vitaly Titov/Shutterstock; 15, Courtesy Sharon Anderson; 16, © AnneMS/Shutterstock; 17, Courtesy Sharon Anderson; 19, Courtesy Pen Ryn Estate; 20, © Babii/Shutterstock; 21, © Mihai_Andritoiu/Shutterstock and © Lana K/Shutterstock; 23, © Kathy D. Reasor/Shutterstock; and 24, © PetlinDmitry/Shutterstock.

President: Jen Jenson
Director of Product Development: Spencer Brinker
Editor: Allison Juda
Designer: Micah Edel
Cover: Kim Jones

Library of Congress Cataloging-in-Publication Data

Names: Markovics, Joyce L., author.
Title: Horror in Pennsylvania / by Joyce Markovics.
Description: Minneapolis, Minnesota : Bearport Publishing Company, [2021] | Series: Scary states (of mind) | Includes bibliographical references and index.
Identifiers: LCCN 2020000519 (print) | LCCN 2020000520 (ebook) | ISBN 9781647470784 (library binding) | ISBN 9781647470883 (ebook)
Subjects: LCSH: Haunted places—Pennsylvania—Juvenile literature. | Ghosts—Pennsylvania—Juvenile literature. | Pennsylvania—Miscellanea—Juvenile literature.
Classification: LCC BF1472.U6 M34348 2021 (print) | LCC BF1472.U6 (ebook) | DDC 133.109748—dc23
LC record available at https://lccn.loc.gov/2020000519
LC ebook record available at https://lccn.loc.gov/2020000520

Copyright © 2021 Bearport Publishing Company. All rights reserved. No part of this publication may be reproduced in whole or in part, stored in any retrieval system, or transmitted in any form or by any means, electronic, mechanical, photocopying, recording, or otherwise, without written permission from the publisher.

For more information, write to Bearport Publishing, 5357 Penn Avenue South, Minneapolis, MN 55419. Printed in the United States of America.

CONTENTS

Horror in Pennsylvania

Pennsylvania is rich in history—and in horror! It's one of the nation's oldest and most haunted states. Explore a battlefield visited by dead soldiers. Check out a spooky prison with an unbelievable past. Get up close with the many scary **spirits** that roam the state.

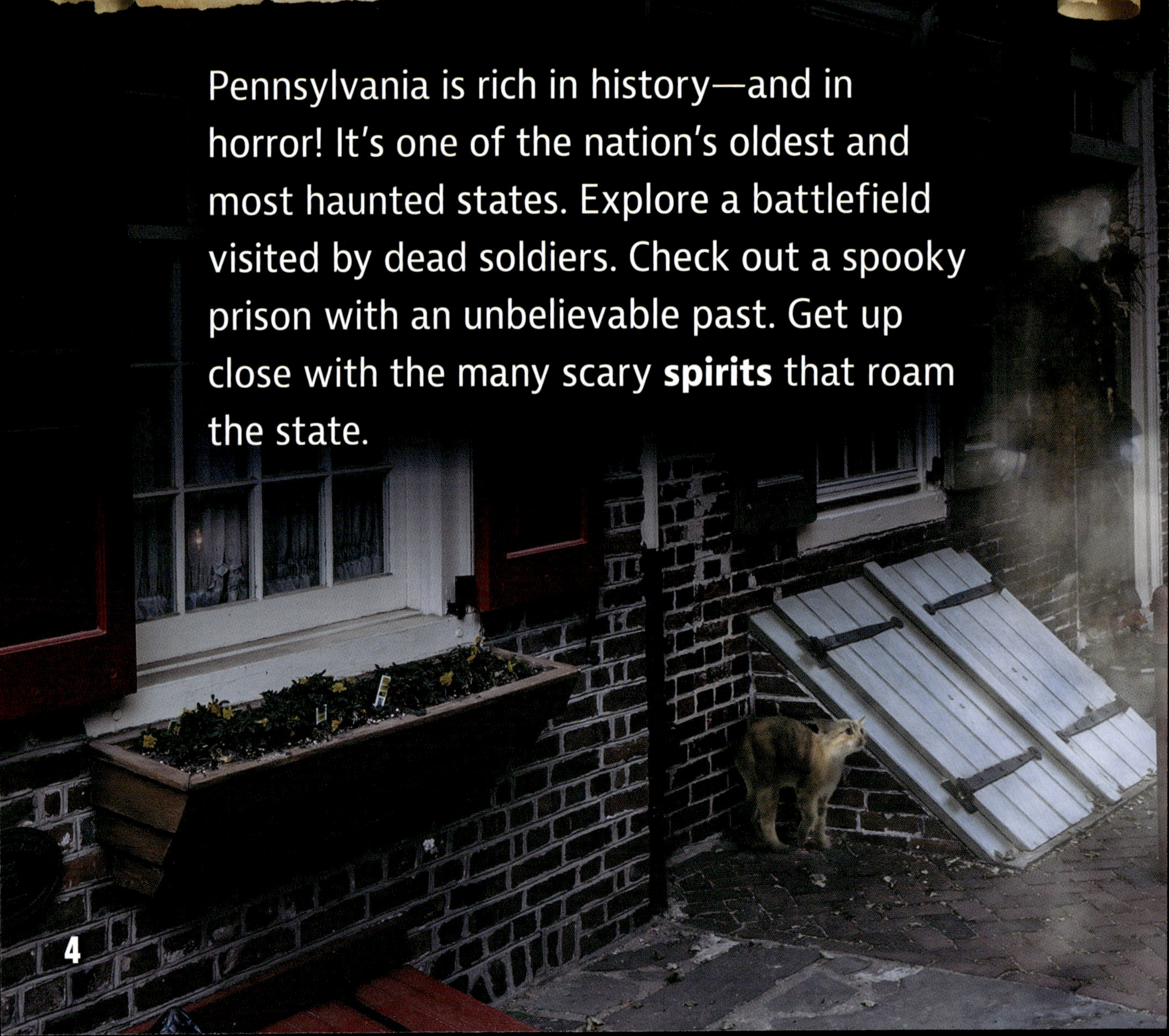

Get ready to read four spooky stories about Pennsylvania. Turn the page . . . if you dare.

Spirit Soldiers

Devil's Den, Gettysburg

Devil's Den is a rocky hill at the edge of Gettysburg. Long ago, locals believed a huge, monsterous snake slithered among the rocks.

Soldiers used Devil's Den during the Battle of Gettysburg in the Civil War (1861–1865). As they hid among the huge **boulders**, they shot and killed their enemies. Many men died there. A nearby creek even turned red with their blood.

The Battle of Gettysburg was the bloodiest battle of the Civil War. Over 50,000 soldiers were killed or wounded.

With so much death at the place, is it a surprise that Devil's Den is haunted? There have been sightings of two men in old, bloodstained uniforms carrying guns. Another spirit at Devil's Den wears ripped clothes and no shoes. Sometimes, he walks up to visitors and says, "What you're looking for is over there." Then, he **vanishes** into thin air!

Tortured Souls

Eastern State Penitentiary, Philadelphia

Eastern State **Penitentiary**, or ESP, has a gruesome history. Some ESP **inmates** were **tortured**. They were dunked in freezing water in the middle of winter until ice covered their skin. Others were strapped in a chair where they were unable to move. Still other prisoners were thrown into a pitch-black cell. Do the spirits of these men haunt the prison even today?

ESP opened as a prison in 1829 and closed in 1971. It's now a museum.

In the 1990s, as a worker named Gary Johnson opened a locked door, an unseen force seized him. Gary was unable to move. Then, he felt a wave of energy rush out of the cell. It was as if an icy hand had reached deep inside him.

When Gary looked up, he saw ghostly faces in **agony** on the walls. He ran away as fast as he could.

Inside the penitentiary

Here, Kitty, Kitty!

Cranberry Manor Bed and Breakfast, East Stroudsburg

The Cranberry Manor Bed and Breakfast welcomes many visitors, including one special guest. People feel it jump on their beds in the morning. It brushes against their legs. It can also be heard running up and down the stairs. Sometimes, it even meows. Meet Missy, the ghost cat of Cranberry Manor!

Cranberry Manor

An earlier owner of Cranberry Manor hated cats. She shooed them from the house. So how do you explain the ghost kitty's **presence**? The inn is also home to the spirit of a little girl. She was upset because she couldn't keep her pet cat in the house. Perhaps now she can.

Sometimes, Cranberry Manor guests wake up to the smell of bacon and coffee when the kitchen is still dark and empty.

IN LOVE AND DEATH

Pen Ryn Estate, Bensalem

Pen Ryn Estate is a grand house that was built in 1744 by businessman Abraham Bickley III. It's said that Abraham's son, Robert, married a woman his father hated. Abraham wouldn't allow his son's bride to enter the house. One December 24, Robert had a fight with his father. He then waded into a nearby river and drowned.

Pen Ryn Estate is located along the Delaware River. This is the river where Robert is said to have drowned.

Pen Ryn Estate

As the story goes, every Christmas Eve, a thin, slimy **corpse** slowly rises from the river. It drags itself to Pen Ryn. Then, the figure taps on the windows with its bony fingers.

Another ghost also appears on the grounds. She is seen riding a big, black horse. The ghost woman screams and disappears into the woods. Is this **phantom** Robert's heartbroken wife?

Spooky Spots in Pennsylvania

Cranberry Manor Bed and Breakfast
Meet the playful ghost cat named Missy.

Pen Ryn Estate
Watch out for angry, lovesick ghosts at this old house.

Eastern State Penitentiary
Explore a spooky prison with a horrible past.

Devil's Den
Come face-to-face with long-dead soldiers.

GLOSSARY

agony (AG-uh-nee) extreme pain or suffering

boulders (BOHL-derz) large rocks

corpse (KORPS) a dead body

inmates (IN-mayts) prisoners

penitentiary (pen-uh-TEN-shuh-ree) a prison

phantom (FAN-tuhm) a ghost or ghostlike image

presence (PREZ-uhns) a person or thing that exists but is not seen

spirits (SPIHR-its) ghosts

tortured (TAWR-cherd) forced to suffer great pain

vanishes (VAN-ish-uhz) disappears from sight

INDEX

READ MORE

Camisa, Kathryn. *Horror Hotels (Tiptoe Into Scary Places).* New York: Bearport (2017).

Rudolph, Jessica. *Ghost Houses (Tiptoe Into Scary Places).* New York: Bearport (2017).

LEARN MORE ONLINE

1. Go to **www.factsurfer.com**
2. Enter "**Horror in Pennsylvania**" into the search box.
3. Click on the cover of this book to see a list of websites.

ABOUT THE AUTHOR

Joyce Markovics has written over 100 books for children. She loves old, spooky places and volunteers as a gravestone cleaner in Ossining, New York.